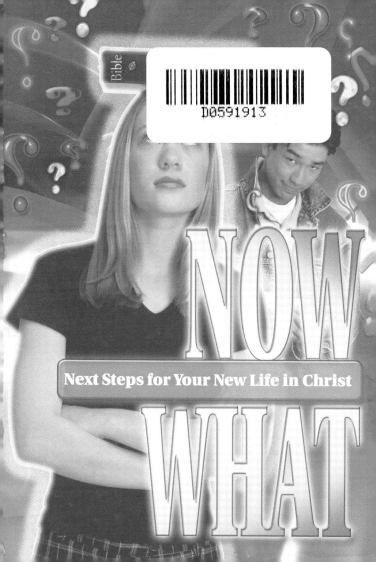

Bible

NOW

Next Steps for Your New Life in Christ

WHAT

Jacob Fasig
Paul Bonner
Dietrich Kirk

NOW

Next Steps for Your New Life in Christ

WHAT

Cover Design: Kelly Chinn

03 04 05 06 07 08 09 10 11 12—10 9 8 7 6 5 4 3 2 1

Contents

Questions
As you read, use the margins to write any questions you have.

The Heavens Are Celebrating

A party is going on in your honor right now. Your new commitment to Christ has caused all of heaven to rejoice and celebrate over you (Luke 15:7). Your decision is more exciting than hitting a grand slam to win the World Series, more exciting than winning a million dollars, and more important than finding a cure for any disease. The most crucial decision in your life has been made. Your name has been written in God's Book of Life, and your invitation to the "party" is in the mail. Now it's time to truly live life; but before we go any farther, let's review what this step means.

In committing your life to Christ, you:

! Recognize that you are a sinner in need of God's grace and forgiveness;

! Repent of your sins—in other words, you're sorry for your sins and will seek God's help in choosing not to sin;

! Believe that Jesus is the Son of God;

! Claim Jesus as your Lord and Savior.

(Know that these statements are not a one-shot deal, but life-long commitments that you will have to continually make. You will have days when claiming Jesus won't be the easiest or most popular thing to do, so you'll have to continually choose Jesus.)

Now that you are beginning to understand your decision, let's talk about what it means for your life.

Questions

You Are Forgiven

The most amazing part about accepting Jesus into your life is God's promise of forgiveness (Matthew 26:28; Acts 13:38). This gift you've been given is called *grace*. Grace is the gift that God gives to you by loving you even when you don't live up to whom God created you to be. It means that you are forgiven of your sins and will spend eternity with God. What a gift! All of the bad things you have done are erased from your record. No amount of money can buy grace, and no act of kindness nor any good works can earn it. Grace is God's grandest

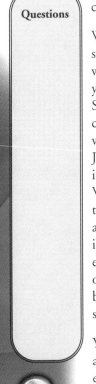

gift to humans through Jesus. And because of this gift, all Christians have new life, a chance to begin again with God.

When you commit your life to Christ, you start living for God instead of yourself. And when you live for God, Christ will reside in your heart (2 Corinthians 5:17). When Scripture says, "in Christ we are a new creation," it means that God is continually working inside us to make us more like Jesus. You are being transformed from the inside out as you become more like Christ. What does that mean? You'll be different in the way you think, different in your attitude, different in what you see as important (your priorities), and maybe even different in the way you act toward others. Even though these changes might be slow and subtle, at some point you will stop and realize that you are different.

You might be asking, "What's so amazing about having forgiveness and grace for eternal life when I'm still struggling in this life?" That's the best part. You are free. Sin and guilt had us bound up in chains, but Jesus broke the chains and allowed us to live freely. You don't have to live under the burden of sin anymore. Jesus washes away our sin so that we are blameless before God. You will still have troubles in this life, but you don't have to be defeated by them. In Christ, you have the victory over temptation; and you have God's strength to get you through hard times. Even if you mess up, God is eager to forgive you again. That's some good news!

God Is With You

Another awesome gift you are given when you choose to follow Christ is the Holy Spirit. You might be asking, "What in the world is that?" The Holy Spirit is how God works in us, helping us on a daily basis to understand more about God and make wise decisions. You can't see the Holy Spirit and you can't taste or smell the Holy Spirit. However, the Spirit is in you and is continually working through you. God is present in your life through the

Questions

9

Questions

Holy Spirit. Having the Holy Spirit is like having a partner or a tour guide to help you along the journey (John 14:16). As you spend more time in prayer and become more like Jesus, the Holy Spirit will become stronger within you.

The Long Road

More than two thousand years ago, a man named Jesus walked this earth. He changed the world by what he taught and how he lived. Many people didn't understand who he was. Even the disciples, who followed him for years, did not understand. Following the events of Jesus' crucifixion, Jesus had to reappear to the disciples to help them believe what he had told them.

Think about that. The disciples, who traveled with Jesus, talked and listened to Jesus, broke bread with Jesus, and even performed miracles with him did not fully understand who he was. And now, two thousand years later, we are supposed to have faith in someone we've never seen or met (John 20:29). But think about this: If we understood all there is to know about God, we wouldn't need God. We'd be able to answer everything ourselves. We will know God fully only when we are united in heaven.

So now you know everything you need to know for a life of faith, right? Not so fast! Everyone has questions. Don't feel that you are the only one. You can get to know God by studying the Bible, praying, finding a Christian friend or mentor to walk with you on your journey, and getting involved in church. As your relationship with God through Jesus Christ deepens, you will find yourself living as Christ lived; and you will long to become more and more like Jesus. When you have questions, ask a pastor or youth pastor, friend in faith, or another adult who models the faith—and always, ask God. Don't ever give up searching or asking questions; don't let a lack of answers keep you from having faith (Jeremiah 29:11, 13). What's important is to let your faith sustain you while you search for the truth.

Questions

11

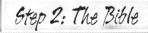

Questions

versions and study Bibles to find the right one for you. You'll find many Bible translations, because Bible scholars are constantly looking for better ways to translate Scriptures into our language. Look for a *New Revised Standard Version* (NRSV), a *New Living Translation* (NLT), a *Contemporary English Version* (CEV), or a *New International Version* of the Bible (NIV). Also, check into some student Bibles. They include explanations of the texts, devotionals, and helpful references. A student Bible will help you understand what you're reading as you read.

In addition, get a devotional book that has stories to help you more fully understand particular Bible passages. You can find many devotional guides at your local Christian bookstore and a list of some great devotionals on page 64—including a book of devotions on the Gospel of John!

Studying your Bible every day is one of the most important things you can do as a young Christian. Try to read every day for 30 days, then it will become a life-changing holy habit.

The next steps in your Christian walk include reading the Bible every day. To hold yourself accountable to this promise, sign and date the statements of commitment. Notice that this time you have two commitments to make (see below and page 22).

Questions

DATE:

I commit to read the Gospel of _____ (Mark or John) over the next 30 days.

SIGNATURE:

21

Questions

DATE: [ ]

I commit to read my Bible
5 minutes every day so that
I can learn more about God
and God's plans for me.

SIGNATURE: [ ]

Psalm 119:105 (NRSV)
Your word is a lamp to my feet and a light
to my path.

(Write a prayer in the form of a letter to God,
telling about what this Scripture passage means
to you. Ask God any questions you might have
about the Bible.)

Questions

**Become Active in Church
and Youth Group**

As a new Christian, you should get connected with a Christian community as soon as possible. Being a Christian is about living in community with other believers. No one can be a strong Christian alone. By actively participating in a church and youth group, you will make wonderful friends; receive education and guidance as a Christian; and best of all, you'll be nurtured into a deeper faith.

In a youth group, you'll be involved with friends who are your age and who are going through the same temptations and struggles that you face. More experienced Christians will be able to help you, and you will be able to help others as well. Talk about valuable support! We all need that extra strength to grow in faith.

The Christian community is made up of many different parts, but each part is needed for the church to be the strongest it can be. By joining the community of faith, you are committing to bring your gifts and offer them to God in service to the community. Think about what you bring to a community:

! What are your gifts and talents?

! How can God use you to build up the church?

Attending church is also important because that is your opportunity to gather with other believers and give praise to God for your life in Jesus Christ. Church is our set-aside time to actively say thanks to God, without the distractions of everyday life. If you're having trouble finding a church home, ask a Christian friend for some suggestions.

Commit yourself to becoming active in a church. Don't try to stand alone as a Christian; walking the road of faith is experienced much more deeply in

Questions

fellowship with other believers. God calls us to be in communion together. This step is vital in your Christian walk, so don't skip it. Your two-part commitment means that you will not only find a church, but also get involved as soon as you can and that you'll jump in to a youth group to experience your faith journey with other believers your own age.

DATE:

I commit to finding and becoming active in a church.

And I will also become an active part of their youth group.

Church Name:

SIGNATURE:

1 Corinthians 12:12, 27 (NIV)
The body is a unit, though it is made up of many parts; and though all its parts are many, they form one body. So, it is with Christ. . . . Now you are the body of Christ, and each one of you is a part of it.

(Write a prayer in the form of a letter to God, telling about what this Scripture passage means to you. Ask God any questions you might have about the church.)

Questions

Setting Christian Priorities

In the space below, write the things that are most important to you in life.

Questions

Now take a minute to think about what you wrote. What did you think of first? Where was God on your list? Now that you have given your life to Christ, he has to be number one. Your first priority is to serve, honor, and live like Jesus. Your priorities should be in the order God wants them to be. Jesus knows what's best for you, so put him first and depend on him for everything else on your list. Make a list of the priorities you think Jesus would want you to have. Don't forget to add anything you left out that he would want there.

Questions

Now, compare your list on page 28 with the one above. You can probably see that you are going to have to make some changes. Jesus would never want you to have popularity, money, or other worldly things high on your list. Jesus wants you to love God, love your family, share your love with others, and be a light to the world.

Now think about the relationships in your life—school, work, sports, parties, friends, family, boyfriend or girlfriend. Now that you've accepted Jesus, where do you need to make changes? How will you act and live in those relationships? How will your love for God be seen in your relationships?

Remember that you are a new creation. You might find it difficult to change your priorities, but God will help you. Pray for the courage to put God first and to let that decision shape every other part of your life. Then know that God is with you and will give you strength to make the right decisions. If you keep Christ first, the other things will fall into place. You will go through times when your priorities get out of whack and so will your life. Just remember to reprioritize and allow Jesus to be Lord of your life again. Life will be better, even in the tough times. Keep yourself accountable to making your relationship with God number one on your list of priorities by signing the statement of commitment below.

Questions

DATE: ⬚

**I commit to making Christ's
priorities my priorities.
I know that this won't be
easy, but I know that God
will help me as I live like
Jesus Christ.**

SIGNATURE: ⬚

NOWWHAT? — Prayer Journal

Questions

Matthew 6:33 (CEV)

More than anything else, put God's work first and do what [God] wants. Then the other things will be yours as well.

(Write a prayer in the form of a letter to God, telling about what this Scripture passage means to you. Ask God any questions you might have about making Christ's priorities your own.)

Let Your Light Shine

Don't hide your commitment; instead, live it out. You are a new creation in Christ, and God called you to be a light to the world. Sometimes when we are unsure or new at something, we are shy or timid about it. But your new life in Jesus Christ is not something to be timid about. Jesus calls us to let our lights shine. What he really means is that we are to let his light shine through us so that everyone can see him working in us.

Unfortunately, we live in a world of sin and darkness. We sometimes find it hard to let the light within us shine through when we are faced with the darkness of temptation and evils all around us. But imagine the feeling of reflecting God's light into bad situations that you've been a part of! Somehow God's light makes even the toughest situation seem brighter. Show everyone your new commitment—not only through your words, but with your life.

Questions

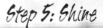

Questions

Every minute counts. Live out your faith while you are with your friends, at a party, playing sports, simply hanging out, and everywhere else. Live for God everywhere and all the time. Whether you are by yourself or in a huge group, be an example of the love and care of Christ Jesus himself. You may be the only light of Christ that other people see. Make it count.

Be strong, and ground yourself in the light of Jesus Christ; because it's always easy to fall back into the old ways. Take comfort that God is with you and that you are not alone. Don't hide; be a light.

This step is not as easy as saying that you'll start reading the Bible or praying every day. You might wonder how to shine Christ's light into the world. As you study the Bible, pray, and learn more about God in church, you will discover that loving others with God's love is the best way to shine.

As you sign the statement of commitment below, you are saying that you will let Christ's love so fill you that it flows from your life into the hearts of others.

Questions

DATE:

I commit to live my life
striving to be a disciple
of Jesus. I will shine
as a light of Jesus Christ
wherever I am.
I will love and serve God
with my life.

SIGNATURE:

Questions

Matthew 5:16 (NRSV)

In the same way, let your light shine before others, so that they may see your good works and give glory to your Father in heaven.

(Write a prayer in the form of a letter to God, telling about what this Scripture passage means to you. Ask God any questions you might have about being a light in the world.)

Tell Another Christian About Your News

We cannot do things alone. Even Jesus took the disciples with him almost everywhere he went. You were created to need companionship—not only with God, but with other believers. By telling a Christian friend about your commitment, you open the door of your heart for support and Christian friendship.

This friend needs to be someone who can hold you accountable to your walk with Christ. Whether this person is your youth pastor, best friend, brother, or sister, you need a relationship of accountability to help guide you along with your new commitment. Without the support of believing friends, you will be tempted much more easily. By entering into Christian friendship, you have someone to help you during times of struggle. This is, by far, the best way to avoid difficult situations that might cause you to compromise your beliefs. If someone else knows what you're struggling with, he or she can be available to you and pray for you.

Questions

By signing this statement of commitment
you are promising to share your news with
a Christian friend and to enter into a
relationship of accountability and support.

Questions

DATE: [ ]

**I commit to enter into an
accountability relationship with**

_____

and to meet together regularly.

Location:

Time:

Day of the Week:

SIGNATURE: [ ]

Proverbs 27:17 (CEV)
Just as iron sharpens iron, friends sharpen
the minds of each other.

(Write a prayer in the form of a letter to God,
telling about what this Scripture passage means
to you. Ask God any questions you might have
about sharing your journey with Christian friends.)

Questions

Questions

Tell Your Family About Your News
This step can definitely be more difficult than most, but it can also be one of the most strengthening. Depending on your family situation, this might be a step that will need extra prayer and planning. Here are some suggestions for whatever your situation:

If you are part of a Christian family—
Be open and honest with your family, and they will nurture you in your new commitment and rejoice with you in your new life. Talk with them about what led you to your decision, and ask for their support as you join them on the Christian journey. Think about having a family devotional time or a Bible study so that you might grow closer as a family and closer to Christ. Commit to talking about your journey with each family member, so you can build up one another and be there for one another.

If you are not part of a Christian family—

Your family may or may not be supportive of your new decision. They may not fully understand the decision you have made. Begin by living out your new commitment so that they can see it. In other words, live a Christian life in your home through your actions—by being loving, forgiving, helping, being compassionate, and so on. Then when you feel comfortable, look for an opportunity to tell your family all about your awesome news. Talk with a trusted friend or youth pastor about how you will tell your family.

However you think your family will react, it is important to tell them. They should know of your commitment to Jesus Christ, because you may be the only light of Christ they ever experience. Don't be scared. God will guide and protect you through this step (Philippians 4:13).

Questions

Step 7: Tell

Questions

Make a commitment to talk with your family about your new life in Christ. Ask them to support you and encourage you as you seek to follow him.

DATE:

I commit to tell my family by this day

_____ (date)

so that they can share with me in the love of Christ.

SIGNATURE:

2 Timothy 1:7-8a (CEV)
God's Spirit doesn't make cowards out of us.
The Spirit gives us power, love, and self-
control. Don't be ashamed to speak for our
Lord.

(Write a prayer in the form of a letter to God,
telling about what this Scripture passage means
to you. Ask God any questions you might have
about telling others.)

Questions

Questions

Living Like Christ

One of the most difficult steps of being a Christian is following Christ daily. When you became a Christian, you made Jesus your Lord and Savior and promised to follow him. Paul, the writer of most of the New Testament, puts it this way: "It is no longer I who live, but it is Christ who lives in me"(Galatians 2:20). As Christ lives through us, we become more and more like him.

One great way to make sure that you are living more like Christ is to continually ask: "What would Jesus do?" This question pertains to all of life. How would Jesus treat people at school? How would Jesus act around people who are drinking or doing drugs? What kind of decisions would Jesus make about sexual intimacy? When faced with these situations, think about what you know of Jesus' life and imitate him. Pray that God will fill you with the knowledge of Christ so that you'll always know how to respond in any situation.

Jesus would love others and honor God in everything; so when you are faced with a question, think about how you can love others and honor God in everything you do. Some things are no-brainers, such as Would God be honored by getting high? No. Other things are not as easy, such as Would God want you to take the better-looking date or the smarter date to the prom? As you learn more about how Jesus lived his life, you'll be able to grow in your ability to follow and serve him. Christ's number one commandment was to love God and love one another as much as he loves us. So go love as many people as you can, with the same love that Christ has given you.

After rising from the dead, Jesus' final commandment to his disciples was to make disciples of all nations (Matthew 28:19-20). Jesus is commanding you to do the same. Don't hide your commitment; live it out.

You are called to live a life after the example of Christ. It will not be an easy thing to do; it wasn't easy for Jesus. But

Questions

Step 8: Imitate

Questions

Jesus will walk with you and guide you by the presence of the Holy Spirit. Make a promise to imitate Christ every day. Jesus Christ was loving, compassionate, kind, prophetic, and honorable. Think about how you can live out these and other characteristics of Jesus.

DATE: [   ]

I commit this day to live a life worthy of my salvation by following Christ every minute of every day. And when I don't live this way, I will ask God for forgiveness and will begin again.

SIGNATURE: [   ]

Galatians 2:19-20 (NRSV)
I have been crucified with Christ; and it is
no longer I who live, but it is Christ who
lives in me. And the life I now live in the
flesh I live by faith in the Son of God.

(Write a prayer in the form of a letter to God,
telling about what this Scripture passage means
to you. Ask God any questions you might have
about imitating Christ.)

Questions

Continually Turn to God:
The Never-Ending Journey

Questions

Being Christian is a never-ending journey. But this step in your life does not mean that you will be perfect. Be prepared to fail, sometimes even more than you succeed. As Christians, our goal is to become like Jesus, formed in his image and example. Jesus will work in us to make us more like him if we make ourselves open to his working. Don't get stuck thinking that you must be perfect. God is and will be perfecting you until you see God face to face in heaven.

During times of struggle, when you are battling temptation, turn to God for help and support. The church is the physical representation of God and a place for help and guidance. God promises to take care of you; you just have to turn to God.

Another way to stay grounded in your faith is to have a daily devotional time. Go to a Christian bookstore and find a devotional guide that works for you. Whether you have a devotional time in the morning or before you go to bed, you cannot imagine what a difference consistent time with God will make. (Look for suggested resources in the back of this book.)

Questions

During good, bad, and all times in between, turn to God (as well as the church) to give you support and courage for the road. Check yourself as time goes by and see how you're doing. Make sure that you are on track with your spiritual journey. If you have leveled off, don't quit. God loves you so much, and the Bible tells us that nothing in this world can separate us from that love (Romans 8:38-39). God will never give up on you, so don't give up on God. Throughout your life, turn to God with all your needs; and the Lord will provide.

Praise God that you have made the decision to follow Christ. You still have a long road to travel, so take the journey one day at a time. Remember that walking by faith means putting one foot in front of the other, with both eyes on God.

NOWWHAT?

Your final commitment (in this book, anyway) is to seek God in everything you do and to grow in your walk with Christ.

Questions

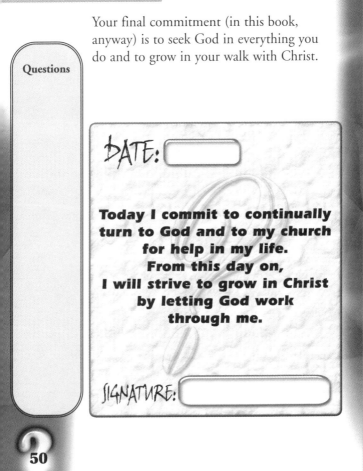

DATE: [   ]

**Today I commit to continually turn to God and to my church for help in my life.
From this day on, I will strive to grow in Christ by letting God work through me.**

SIGNATURE: [   ]

Romans 8:38-39 (NRSV)

For I am convinced that . . . [nothing] will be able to separate us from the love of God in Christ Jesus our Lord.

Questions

(Write a prayer in the form of a letter to God, telling about what this Scripture passage means to you. Ask God any questions you might have about living for Christ.)

Snapshot Glossary of Confusing Words

Questions

Baptism: A way that God marks us as God's own. We are baptized by water as a sign that God is washing away all our sin and giving us new life in Christ.

Disciple: A person who seeks to follow Jesus Christ in everyday life, above everything else

Faith: Your belief and trust in God

Grace: God's undeserved gift of forgiveness, which gives us salvation and is freely offered to everyone

Holy Communion (also known as Eucharist and Lord's Supper):
A ceremony to celebrate and remember Jesus' sacrifice on the cross and the grace and forgiveness of sins that it brings. The celebration is a commemoration of Jesus' Last Supper with his disciples.

Holy Spirit: God's vessel through which God instructs all believers; the third person of the Trinity

Prayer: A conversation with God—listening to God; sharing joys, concerns, trials, and love through talking with God

Rededication: Act of recommitting your life to following Christ, turning away from sin

Sacrament: A ritual in the church. The two sacraments in most churches are baptism and Communion. Sacraments are ways of receiving God's grace in our lives.

Salvation: Being put into a right relationship with God through our belief in the life, death, and resurrection of Jesus Christ

Saved: (see *Salvation*)

Trinity: The Divine union; God the Father, Jesus Christ the Son, and the Holy Spirit; God in three persons

Questions

Questions

Prayer is not something that can be done only one way. People pray in many different ways. The only wrong way to pray is not doing it at all. You cannot be wrong when you open yourself to God. Just follow your heart, and do a lot of listening to your heart. A few patterns for prayer are listed here. Try not to worry about whether you're doing it right.

Prayer might take a while to get used to, but keep at it. God is waiting to talk to you—just be available. Finally, take your time in prayer; don't worry, God doesn't have anywhere else to be except with you. May the peace of God be with you as you learn to pray.

The Breath Prayer

The breath prayer is a really short prayer that can be said in the time it takes you to inhale and exhale. This style of prayer can very easily be incorporated into your daily life, even while you're walking the halls at school.

Here are some suggested breath prayers:

"God, give me your guidance."

"God, grant me patience."

"God, make me an example of your love."

"God, give me strength."

"Lord, make me a blessing."

If none of these suggestions work for you, make up your own breath prayer. This type of prayer will really help you focus on God throughout your day! You can also use the breath prayer to pray for other people.

Questions

PRAY Prayer

Another great way to pray is the PRAY form of prayer:

P raise: Give thanks for the many ways God has entered into your life, giving help when you need it and grace when you don't deserve it. Praise is joyful!

R epent: Repent means to turn around, or change direction. Ask forgiveness. Repent of errors and poor judgment. Repent of things you have done that you shouldn't have. Just as you can turn around physically, you can change direction in your spiritual life and behavior.

A sk (for Others): As a follower of Jesus, care about others as he did. Pray for the needs of others—family, friends, church, community, people you don't know personally, the world.

Y ourself: Like a really close friend, God wants to be with you. Pray about your hurts and fears, express your needs and desires, and seek strength and guidance in all things.

All-Day Prayer

Have a conversation with God that starts in the morning and goes all day long until you go to bed. The way to do this is to start your prayer in the morning; but don't say, "Amen." Let your prayer go all day, saying little prayers for friends and enemies, strength, forgiveness, patience, those around you, or anything else you can think of. With this form of prayer, you are living a prayer all day. Then before you go to sleep, take a minute to reflect in silence. Let God talk to you. Thank God for the gift of your day. Close with an "amen." Then you are ready to start again in the morning. Be open for God to work in your life by being in a constant attitude of prayer.

Questions

Prayer Journal

Use these pages to begin your prayer life with God. You might want to write prayers as letters, as poems, or as conversations. Also write what you think God might be saying to you.

Resources

Bibles

○ *New International Version* (NIV) *Teen Study Bible* (Zondervan, 1999), ISBN: 0310900964. (Hardcover), 0310903947 (Paperback)

○ *NIV Teen Devotional Bible: Devotions for Teens Written by Teens* (Zondervan, 1999), ISBN: 0310916542.

○ *Extreme Faith Compact Youth Bible* (Contemporary English Version [CEV]) (American Bible Society, 2000), ISBN: 1585161683.

○ *The Spiritual Formation Bible* (NRSV) (Zondervan, 1999) ISBN: 0310900891.

Devotionals

○ *I Am Not Ashamed: 50 Devotions for Teens on Romans,* by Laurie Polich (Dimensions for Living, 2003), ISBN: 0687081181.

○ *Dive Into Living Water: 50 Devotions for Teens on the Gospel of John,* by Laurie Polich (Dimensions for Living, 2002), ISBN: 0687052238.

○ *365 Meditations for Teens* (Dimensions for Living, 2000), ISBN: 0687088070.

○ *Way to Live: Christian Practices for Teens* (Upper Room, 2002), ISBN: 0835809757.

○ *Devo'Zine* (devotional magazine designed just for youth): To subscribe, call 800-925-6847 or go online at *www.upperroom.org/devozine.*

Websites

○ *www.devozine.org*
○ *www.waytolive.org*